Grow Your Own

Lettuce

Helen Lanz

SEA-TO-SEA

Mankato Collingwood London

To Anna, for the first seeds we sowed together

This edition first published in 2012 by
Sea-to-Sea Publications
Distributed by Black Rabbit Books
P.O. Box 3263, Mankato, Minnesota 56002

Copyright © Sea-to-Sea Publications 2012

Printed in China

9 8 7 6 5 4 3 2

Published by arrangement with the Watts Publishing Group Ltd, London.

Library of Congress Cataloging-in-Publication Data

Lanz, Helen.
 Lettuce / by Helen Lanz.
     p. cm. -- (Grow your own)
 Includes index.
 ISBN 978-1-59771-311-5 (library binding)
 1. Lettuce--Juvenile literature. 2. Vegetable gardening--Juvenile literature. I. Title.
 SB351.L6L36 2012
 635'.52--dc22
                        2011001219

Series editor: Sarah Peutrill
Art director: Jonathan Hair
Design: Jane Hawkins
Photography: Victoria Coombs/Ecoscene (unless otherwise credited)

Credits: Carmen Martínez Banús/istockphoto: front cover b. Barbro Bergfeldt/istockphoto: 8b.
Mariya Bibikova/istockphoto: front cover inset, 25b. Peter Etchells/SPL: 16t. Invisible/Shutterstock:
front cover t. Helen Lanz: 14b, 17t, 21tr, 24b, 26b. MM Productions/Corbis: 6b. Juan Monino/
istockphoto: 7b, 29. T Ranger/istockphoto: 14cr. Cappi Thompson/istockphoto: 27. Ed Young/
AgstockUSA/SPL: 18b.
Every attempt has been made to clear copyright. Should there be any inadvertent omission please
apply to the publisher for rectification.

Thanks to Jasmine Clarke and Tony Field for kindly sharing their gardening knowledge.
The author and publisher would like to thank the models who took part in this book.

February 2011
RD/6000006415/001

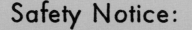

Safety Notice:

Gardening is fun! There are a few basic rules you
should always follow, however. Always garden
with an adult; wear appropriate clothing and
footwear; and always wash your hands when you
have finished in the garden.

Contents

Words in **bold** are in the glossary on page 29.

Why Grow Your Own Lettuce?

▲ You don't need to have a lot of space to grow vegetables (above). But be prepared to enjoy some fresh air! ▼

Have you ever thought about growing your own fruit or vegetables? Well, why not give lettuce a try?

Full of Freshness

Lettuce that you have grown yourself usually has a lot of flavor—and you can't beat it for freshness!

Quick Growing

Lettuce is a really good vegetable to grow. It grows quickly and there are lots of different **varieties**, which have different colors, leaf shapes, and flavors.

▲ Attractive and tasty!

Top Tip!

When growing your own, it is a good idea to keep a growing diary, or notebook. Write down everything you do, from the variety of lettuce you grow, to how and when you do things. This will help if you decide to do it again, and will be fun to look back on, especially if you take pictures of your lettuce as it grows.

Outer leaves

Heart

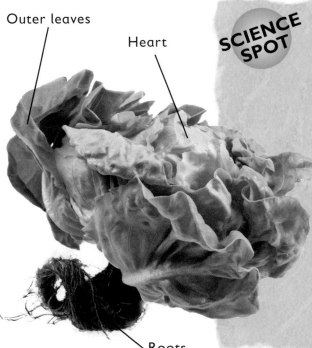

Roots

SCIENCE SPOT

Parts of a Lettuce

The heart, or center of the lettuce: the leaves are smaller and tightly packed together.

The outer leaves: these are larger and looser.

The **root** system: the roots take up water and food from the soil and feed them to the plant's leaves, through its veins, to help the lettuce grow.

What Type of Lettuce?

When you are planning which lettuces to grow, it might be useful to think about the different types of lettuce that there are.

What Kind?

There are four types of lettuce: crisphead, butterhead, looseleaf, and romaine lettuce.

▲ *There are many varieties of lettuce. Some are easier to grow than others.*

Crisphead Lettuce

Crisphead lettuce is, as its name describes, a crisp lettuce that forms a tight ball, or head, of leaves. It doesn't like hot weather and can be more difficult to grow than the other types of lettuce.

▶ *Crisphead lettuce is also called iceberg lettuce.*

Butterhead Lettuce

Butterhead lettuce has a softer, smaller head of looser leaves than the crisphead. Some people describe it as having a light, "buttery" flavor.

▶ *Boston and bibb lettuces are good examples of butterhead lettuce.*

▲ *Looseleaf varieties, such as lollo rossa and salad bowl, can be very colorful lettuces.*

Looseleaf Lettuce

Looseleaf lettuces have open leaves that do not form a head. There are many varieties that can have smooth or frilly leaves in different shapes. The leaves can be green, red, or bronze, making them very attractive to grow.

Looseleaf lettuces tend to grow quickly and are easy to look after.

Romaine Lettuce

Romaine lettuce grows straight upright, with a center of folded leaves. It reached the West from Rome via France, and so it has the name "romaine."

▶ *Romaine lettuce forms the base of a Caesar salad.*

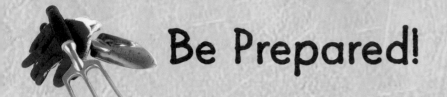

Be Prepared!

Having planned to grow your own, it is worth thinking about what you will need so you can be prepared.

All About You…

You will be outside a lot, so you will need some old clothes that your mom and dad won't mind if you get dirty. Don't forget about your feet. Rubber boots or some old running shoes will do.

… And Your Lettuce, Too

And don't forget to think about what you will need to grow your lettuce.

Probably the most important thing will be lettuce **seeds**!

▶ You can buy your lettuce seeds from a garden center, or by mail order on the Internet.

▶ Egg cartons, homemade seed pots, or seed trays can be useful.

What Else?

A watering can is very important so you can keep your lettuce watered.

You will need a trough, a large plant pot, or a hanging basket to grow your lettuce in if you are not planning to grow it in the ground.

And, of course, if you are growing your lettuce in a container, you will need some soil or **potting mix**.

▼ If you do not have a watering can, you could use a jug instead.

▲ A trowel like this is great, but you can use an old spoon. Check with your carer that it is old before you take it!

◀ Looseleaf lettuces of different colors look lovely in a hanging basket, trough, or pot.

Sow the Seeds

Lettuce can be planted from spring to summer (see page 28). Some varieties can be planted in winter. Check the seed pack for details of when to **sow** your chosen seeds.

Inside or Out?

Lettuce are quite **hardy** little plants, so you could plant them straight outside (see page 15), or you may choose to start growing them on a windowsill indoors. You can plant the seeds in **seedling** pots or trays and transfer them to their final growing spot later.

Top Tip!

For indoor seeds, be careful that they do not grow too quickly and become "leggy" (tall and spindly).
To prevent this, plant the seeds well apart so they do not fight for light.

◄ *Space your seeds well so they have room to grow.*

Step-by-Step

1. Fill your container with potting mix.

2. Lightly water the mix. It is often a good idea to leave this overnight to allow the soil to settle.

3. Now you are ready to plant your seeds! Press two or three seeds into each pot.

4. Gently cover the seeds with some fresh potting mix (just over half an inch/1 cm will do). Firmly but gently press it down.

5. Now give your seeds a drink.

6. If keeping indoors, place on a windowsill where it is warm but not too sunny.

◀ *You can make seedling pots from newspaper or the bottom of an egg carton.*

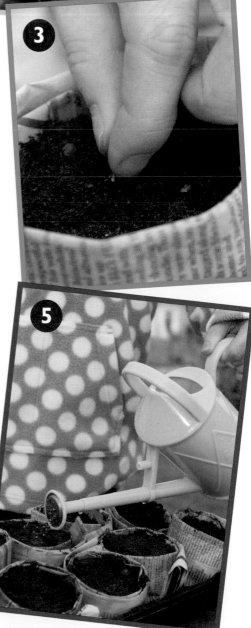

13

Sowing Outside

You may decide to go for the great outdoors right away!

Wait for the Frost

Lettuce is happy in cold, damp conditions and can withstand a little **frost**, so you could plant your seeds outside right away. However, before you sow your seeds, be sure that the main frosts are over.

Wherever you sow, choose a shady spot; lettuce is not happy in full sun.

▼ *The normal time of the last main frost depends on where you live. You can check the Internet for local information.*

▲ *You could sift the soil through a plant pot to remove all the big lumps.*

Lose the Lumps

Lettuce seeds have tiny root systems, so you need to prepare the soil well, whether growing in pots or the ground. The soil needs to be **well-drained**, and damp but not soggy. Give the ground a good digging over before planting.

Step-by-Step

1. To sow into a **bed**, make a **trench** 1 inch (2 cm) deep in the soil. Try to keep it straight. You can use string to help you keep your trench straight by tying it to two sticks, one at each end of your trench.

2. Spread the seeds evenly and thinly in the trench. If you are growing a looseleaf lettuce, you can sow a few more seeds at a time to get a good thick mix of leaves.

3. If you have more than one row of seeds, keep the rows about 12 inches (30 cm) apart.

4. Cover the seeds gently but firmly with soil and give them a drink of water.

Top Tip!

Plant a few seeds at two-week intervals. This means that your lettuce will be ready at different times so you will have a constant supply of lettuce, rather than harvesting it all at once. This is called successional planting.

Under Cover!

If you are planting your lettuce seeds outside near the beginning of the growing season, when it is still cold at night, you may need to cover your seeds.

▲ Place the row cover carefully so the lettuce seeds have room to grow.

Row Covers

Row covers are plastic tunnels that protect seeds from the cold. You can make these using a clear plastic, 64 fl. oz. (2 l) plastic beverage bottle.

Simply wash the bottle out, ask a grown-up to cut off the top and bottom, and then cut the bottle in half lengthwise.

▶ Be sure a grown up helps you to cut the bottles.

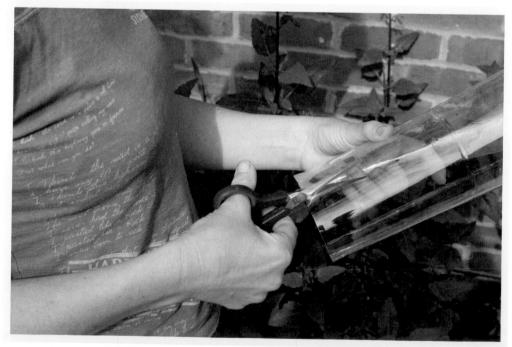

Trapping the Sun

Now carefully place the bottle over your seeds. The row cover lets the light and warmth of the sun's rays through the plastic and traps the warmth—just like a greenhouse does—allowing the seed to grow.

▲ Lettuces will need a little protection if you plant them early in the growing season.

◄ Imagine—these tiny seeds will grow to be big lettuces!

SCIENCE SPOT *What Is a Seed?*

Seeds hold the ingredients for life! The ingredients can wait for years, encased in the seed shell, before they grow, waiting until the conditions are right. Most seeds need darkness, warmth, and water in order to **germinate**. Seeds can be so tiny you can barely see them, or they can be as big as a coconut!

Encouraging Growth

Now you've planted your seeds, it's very important to check them regularly.

The First Shoots!

After about 7–14 days, you will see little **shoots** appearing.

▲ It's exciting to see the little green shoots emerging!

◄ Germinating seeds. The photograph is bigger than real life to show this clearly.

SCIENCE SPOT

Germination

Germination is the point when a seed starts to grow, breaking out of its seed case. The seed stays dormant, or asleep, until water is added. Once water is absorbed, or taken into the seed case, the "baby" plant starts to feed on stored food supplies in the seed case and begins to grow. The root is usually the first thing to break through the seed case, then the first leaves, or **cotyledons**, appear.

▲ Remember to check just below the top of the soil, to make sure it is not just damp on the surface.

Top Tip!

Don't worry if nothing seems to be happening! If you have started your seeds outside, they may take a little longer to come up. Because it is colder outside, the seeds may not germinate as quickly as those inside. Keep watering—but not too much! Feel the soil with your finger. If the soil sticks to your finger, it is damp and the plant doesn't need more water.

Thinning Out

As your seedlings come up, you can "thin out" the young plants if they are crowded in their pot or row. This means pulling up any seedlings that look weaker in order to give the healthier ones more room to grow.

▶ By pulling out the weaker plants, you give the stronger seedlings more chance to develop into healthy lettuces.

Preparing Pot or Plot

When your seedlings have four leaves, they are ready to be planted on into a larger container or bed in the garden. Choose a bed in a warm, but shady, position.

▲ *Your seedlings need planting on so they have more room to grow.*

▶ *Add manure or compost to the soil in the new bed before planting out the seedlings.*

Hardening Off

If you have grown your seedlings inside, it is a good idea to get them used to being outside before you plant them out. To do this, place the seedling pots outside during the day, bringing them in at night. Do this for a couple of days. This is called "hardening off."

Step-by-Step

1. With your trowel, or spoon, make a hole in the soil you have prepared in your pot or bed.

2. Remove the newspaper pot. Gently knock away some of the soil but leave some around the plant's roots. Place the seedling, soil, and roots in the hole.

3. If you have used an egg carton, use your spoon to gently scoop your seedling out. Be careful to lift it with a lump of soil around the seedling so you don't damage the roots.

4. Fill around the roots with fresh soil and press down firmly and gently. Be careful not to bury the leaves.

5. Now repeat this until all the seedlings are planted. Be sure to leave 8–10 inches (20–25 cm) at least between the plants. Looseleaf lettuce seedlings can be closer.

Top Tip!

If you need to handle the seedling, make sure you hold it, gently, by the leaves and not the stem. The stem is so delicate it will snap.

Pests and Problems!

Sometimes **pests** and **diseases** can cause problems! The best way to avoid them is by looking after your crops well.

Tending Your Crop

You will need to keep your lettuces well watered, but not waterlogged, and free from weeds and pests, especially if your lettuces are in the ground.

◄ Removing dead leaves and weeds from around the lettuce plants helps to keep them healthy.

Slugs Are Pests!

There are a number of ways to tackle slippery slugs. You can pick them off your lettuces every evening and get rid of them. You can put crushed egg shells or sand around your lettuce patch, which discourages them from slithering toward your plants. Or, if your lettuces are in containers, smear petroleum jelly around the rim, which also makes it difficult for them to slither across!

Beat the Birds

If birds take a shine to your plants, place mesh or netting around your lettuce or make your own bird scarer.

◄ Old CDs sparkle as the sun hits them when they blow around in the wind. This scares birds away.

Other Problems

Some problems, such as **greenfly**, may need an **insecticide**. **Mildew** or **mold** mean you will need to pull up the plant and throw it away.

► The best way to stop mold (pictured) or mildew is by weeding well and getting rid of dead leaves from around the bottom of your lettuce.

Get Ready for Harvest

You are now building up to the big day when your lettuce will be ready to harvest!

Lovely Leaves

It is the leaves of a plant that help it to grow. The leaves use sunlight, water, and the gas carbon dioxide from the air to make a store of energy to help the plant get bigger. Leaves also help to keep the plant cool in hot weather. The veins in the leaves take the water and **nutrients** from the roots to the leaves.

Vein

Happy Harvesting

Looseleaf lettuces can be ready just eight weeks after sowing. All types of lettuce are ready from between 10 to 14 weeks after sowing.

◀ Picking the lettuce as soon as it is fully grown means it will be fresh, crunchy, and full of flavor.

Harvest your lettuces when they look fully grown, but while they are still young. To harvest looseleaf lettuce, pick the outer leaves, leaving the center ones to continue to grow. This is called "cut-and-come-again" growing.

▶ If you don't pick your lettuce when it's ready, it may "bolt," or continue to grow upward.

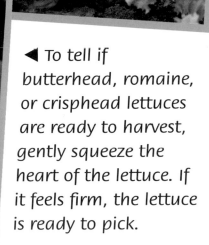

◀ To tell if butterhead, romaine, or crisphead lettuces are ready to harvest, gently squeeze the heart of the lettuce. If it feels firm, the lettuce is ready to pick.

As soon as the heart is formed in butterhead, romaine, and crisphead lettuces, they are ready to be harvested. Cut them at the root and pull off the outer leaves.

Don't forget to enjoy the moment!

Lovely Lettuce

Lettuce is a tasty food that can be enjoyed in many ways. It's good for you too! It contains **vitamins** A, C, and K and betacarotene, which helps your body fight diseases.

▲ *There are so many types of lettuce—if you don't like one type, try another!*
▼ *You can use lettuce to make a tasty side dish with many meals.*

Preparing your Lettuce

Before you get creative with you lettuce, you need to chop off the roots and then wash the leaves well in cold water.

Lettuce Recipes

Lettuce is usually served cold, as part of a salad, but you can also roast lettuce, or use it in soups or **risottos**! You could use large salad leaves instead of tortillas to make crunchy wraps for chicken or make "cups" to hold stir-fries. Why not try the recipe opposite, or search the Internet for more ideas?

Chicken Caesar Salad

Ask an adult to help you with the chopping and cooking parts.

Ingredients
4 slices of Italian bread
3 tablespoons olive oil
1 large romaine lettuce
2 skinless cooked chicken breasts
4 strips bacon
Small block of parmesan cheese, grated

For the Dressing
1 garlic clove
5 tbsp mayonnaise
1 tbsp white wine vinegar

1. Set the oven to 400°F (180°C). Tear the bread into big chunks and spread out on a cookie sheet. Drizzle 2 tablespoons of olive oil over the bread and bake it for 8–10 minutes. These are your croutons.

2. Chop the cooked chicken into big chunks.

3. Fry the bacon in a skillet with the rest of the olive oil until crisp.

4. Bash garlic with the back of a wooden spoon; peel off skin. Crush with a garlic crusher. Mix all of the dressing ingredients. Season with salt and pepper. Your dressing should be the consistency of yogurt. If it's thicker, add a few drops of water.

5. Tear the lettuce into large pieces and arrange in a bowl. Add most of the chicken, bacon, croutons, and grated parmesan. Add most of the dressing. Toss the salad in a bowl. Scatter the remaining chicken, bacon, croutons, and dressing on the top. Sprinkle on the parmesan. Enjoy!

Gardening Calendar

Here's an "at-a-glance" guide to the growing year. Planting and growing times vary, depending on where you live, but you can follow these general guidelines.

Early Winter
(Dec–Jan)

Early winter crop ready for harvest at the beginning of this period.

Late Winter
(Jan–Feb)

For an early crop, sow indoors in pots late on in this period.

Early Spring
(March–April)

Plant out the early crop at beginning of this period under row covers. Sow summer crops outside.

Spring crop ready for harvest toward the end of this period.

Late Spring
(April–May)

Sow summer crops outside.

Harvest early crop.

Early Summer
(June–July)

Sow summer crops outside.

Harvest early crop. Harvest summer crop.

Late Summer
(July–August)

Sow seeds indoors in pots. Sow early winter crop at end of this period.

Early Fall
(Sept–Oct)

Cover early winter crop with row covers. Sow spring crop toward the end of this period under row covers.

Harvest summer crop.

Late Fall
(Oct–Nov)

Early winter crop ready for harvest.

Gardening Glossary

bed: in gardening terms, this means the area of soil for planting seeds.

cotyledon: the first leaves to come from a seed.

diseases: illnesses that can be caught by plants and animals.

frost: frozen water droplets that freeze on the ground on cold mornings.

germinate: the point when a root and leaf break through a seed case and the seed begins to grow.

greenfly: a tiny green fly. It gathers on plants in large numbers and damages the plants.

hardy: strong; in terms of a plant, can withstand the cold, for example.

insecticide: something, usually a spray, used to kill insects.

mildew: tiny fungi that grow, in this case, on plants.

mold: tiny fungi, often furry, that grow in warm, damp conditions.

nutrients: something that gives goodness and nourishment needed for growing or being healthy.

pests: insects or animals that are destructive to the plant, such as slugs or greenfly.

potting mix: a mixture of soil, nutrients, and fertilizer used to feed plants to help them grow.

risotto: an Italian recipe made from rice and other ingredients.

root: the part of a plant below the ground that takes water and nutrients, or goodness, from the soil to the rest of the plant.

seed: a tiny thing that a plant can grow from.

seedling: the young plant grown from a seed.

shoots: new growth from a plant or seed.

sow: to plant seeds.

trench: a small ditch in the soil to plant the seeds in.

varieties: types of a plant.

vitamins: natural substances that are in food that are good for your body and health.

well-drained: to allow water to seep out of the soil, by using rocks or stones, so that the soil doesn't get too wet and soggy.

Index

Useful Web Sites

www.kidsgardening.org/
The National Gardening Association believes that when you garden you grow. Their comprehensive gardening resource web site for children is highly inspirational for all young gardeners.

http://home.howstuffworks.com/ lettuce1.htm
Information about growing your own lettuce, including handy tips and recipes.

www.bbc.co.uk/digin/lettuce.shtml
Fun, animated clip on how to grow lettuce from seeds.

Gardening Club

Have you enjoyed growing your own? How about joining a gardening club? Your school may have one. You could grow fruit and vegetables, or perhaps make ladybug homes to help attract them to your garden. If your school doesn't have a gardening club, why not talk to your teacher about setting one up?

Note to parents and teachers: Every effort has been made by the Publishers to ensure that these web sites are suitable for children, that they are of the highest educational value, and that they contain no inappropriate or offensive material. However, because of the nature of the Internet, it is impossible to guarantee that the contents of these sites will not be altered. We strongly advise that Internet access is supervised by a responsible adult.